AF573678

The Wit of the Wig

THE WIT OF THE WIG

Compiled by

Richard Fountain

LESLIE FREWIN : LONDON

First published in 1968 by
Leslie Frewin Publishers Limited,
15 Hay's Mews, Berkeley Square, London W1

This book has been set in 12 on 14 point Bembo
Printed by Anchor Press
and bound by William Brendon,
both of Tiptree, Essex

09 087630 X

Introduction

'THE LAW IS an ass,' Crippen once remarked; and although I should hardly wish to be so entirely dismissive of the institution and its profession, I for long suspected that a fugitive element, at least of the risible, could occasionally be discerned in our courts. Now, long but never weary hours of research and collection have confirmed that suspicion. This book is the result.

Every anthology, however painstakingly compiled, suffers inevitably from one insurmountable difficulty: there is simply never enough room for everything that one would wish to include. Particularly has this been my trouble on the present occasion. So many times, thumbing through dusty volumes in some quiet law library, I have savoured the sharp and intricate back-and-forth of counsel and witness, the dry comments of the judge – but how in the name of the Lord Gardiner can one contain more than a few of these lengthy passages, replete as they are with wit but in fact culminating in no specific punch line? Well, I have included one or two passages just to give the flavour of such occasions. There again, so many of the examples of wit which kind legal friends have passed on to me have depended for their appreciation upon a working knowledge of the law. As I hoped that even the most lay of laymen would enjoy this collection I have cut out any instance that depended too heavily upon professional knowledge.

Faced, therefore, by the complexities of choice, I have tried to make as catholic a selection as space allows. I have tried to communicate as many as possible of the varieties of flavour of wit – the incisive retort, the bland judicial question, the delicate play on words, the biting or sarcastic quip, the bizarre contrasts between the gruesome details of the case and the cool insouciance of counsel.

During the compilation of this volume two thoughts have frequently arisen in my mind: firstly, that in a curious way the law is no less impressive in human terms for the occasional unintentional lapse into levity; and secondly, that the standards of no human institution are higher than those of British justice.

Finally, if this compilation gives as much pleasure in reading as it gave me in assembling, I shall be amply rewarded.

Richard Fountain

Lord Asquith (1890–1954)

The intellectual atmosphere of the Court of Appeal is one of extreme, of almost Himalayan, rarefaction. One would hardly be surprised if an abominable snowman entered the court and applied for security for costs. . . .

*   *   *

Lord Atkin (1867–1944)

If in 1815 the common law halted outside the banker's door, by 1879 equity had had the courage to lift the latch, walk in and examine the books.

Commenting upon the liberty of the subject in wartime, in a dissenting speech:

In this case I have listened to arguments which might have been addressed acceptably to the Court of King's Bench in the time of Charles I . . . I know of only one authority which might justify the suggested method of construction: 'When I use a word,' Humpty Dumpty said in a rather scornful tone, 'it means just what I choose it to mean, neither more nor less.'

'The question is,' said Alice, 'whether you can make words mean so many different things.'

'The question is,' said Humpty Dumpty, 'which is to be master – that's all.'

* * *

Mr Justice Avory (1851–1935)

When at the bar, Mr Justice Avory was once opposed by a counsel who quoted him a text from the book of Job.

Said Avory gravely:

That evidence is not admissible, seeing that you cannot put Job in the box and prove it.

On enquiring of a witness whether in fact he had previously been convicted:

WITNESS: Yes, sir, but it was due to the incapacity of my counsel rather than to any fault on my part.

MR JUSTICE AVORY (with a smile): It always is, and you have my sincere sympathy.

WITNESS: And I deserve it, seeing as you were my counsel on that occasion.

* * *

Mr Justice Bayley (1763–1841)

While summing up to the jury, he one day rebuked counsel, who was talking in court rather loudly, by saying to him:

Mr X, if ever you arrive here, which some of these days I hope you will do so, you will know the inconvenience of counsel talking while you are summing up.

* * *

Lord Birkenhead (1872–1930)

Lord Birkenhead (then F E Smith) had a particular dislike of being told by judges that they had a poor opinion of his case. One such judge said to him: 'I have read your case, Mr Smith, and I am no wiser now than I was when I started':

Possibly not, my lord, but far better informed.

In a case concerning a taxi collision, the question arose of identifying the taxi as it drove along. The witness for the plaintiff, against FE [as he was always known], was trying to prove that he could identify the taxi and was recalling different features about it which could not possibly have been noticed by the keenest observer. He claimed to recall the colour, the make, the badge, the condition of the hood, the shape of the horn and similar features. FE rose and asked sarcastically:

You did not happen to notice by any chance what fare was marked up on the taximeter?

In an accident case he sympathetically cross-examined a boy whose right arm was alleged to have been crippled by the negligence of the defendant omnibus company:

FE: Will you show me just how high you can lift your arm?

The boy showed in his face the pain it cost him to bring his arm up to the level of his shoulder:

FE: Thank you and now will you show me how high you could lift it before the accident?

Immediately the arm shot up above the head. The case was over.

In one of his early cases he had the following encounter with Mr Justice Ridley:

Mr Smith, I have read your pleadings, and I do not think much of your case.

I am sorry to hear that, my lord (*Smith replied*). But your lordship will find that the more you hear of it the more it will grow on you.

He once differed from a judge on a point of procedure. Despite mounting displeasure on the bench, FE stood his ground until the judge exclaimed:

What do you think I am on the bench for, Mr Smith?

It is not for me (*FE replied gravely*) to attempt to fathom the inscrutable workings of Providence.

While appearing for a tramway company against whom an action had been brought by a boy who had been run over and blinded:

JUDGE: Poor boy, poor boy, stand him on a chair and let the jury see him.

This unjudicial sympathy was prejudicial to FE's case:

FE: Perhaps your honour would like to have the boy passed round the jury box?

JUDGE: That is a most improper remark.

FE: It was provoked by a most improper suggestion.

JUDGE (*furiously*): Mr Smith, have you ever heard of a saying by Bacon, the great Bacon, that youth and discretion are ill-wedded companions?

FE: I have, and have you ever heard the saying of Bacon, the great Bacon, that a much-talking judge is like an ill-tuned cymbal?

JUDGE: You are extremely offensive, young man.
FE: As a matter of fact we both are; the difference between us is that I am trying to be, and you can't help it.

I, my lords, can only express my amazement that men of saintly lives, men of affairs, men whose opinions and experience we respect, should have concentrated upon adultery as the one circumstance which ought to afford relief from the marriage tie.

We have the highest authority for believing that the meek shall inherit the earth; though I have never found any particular corroboration of this aphorism in the records of Somerset House.

If one goes to Scotland, and in making a speech says 'English', the whole audience shouts out 'British'; but if one described Edinburgh as a 'British' city he would not leave it alive.

The speech of the noble and learned lord, as a constructive effort of statecraft, would have been immature upon the lips of a hysterical schoolgirl.

Poor advocates always call great advocates bad lawyers. It somehow seems to equalise things.

I do not deal with subtleties; I am only a lawyer.

I remember that once I had occasion, after I had attained the high office of Lord Chancellor, to go to some races, the name of which I have forgotten, near Dublin. I went in respectable company because I was taken there by the Lord Chancellor of Ireland, so that there were two of us to balance the levity of one another. The advice of my noble colleague – extremely dependable on matters of law – was far less valuable when addressed to the topics of the turf and the result was unfortunate.

I do not know of any single department of life in which men still maintain undisputed supremacy unless it is cooking and women's fashions.

The expression, either in public or private life, that 'something must be done' is the hallmark of weak and undecided people who have not the slightest idea what ought to be done, or why it ought to be done.

Love letters are always kept by a woman unless they are deeply compromising to herself. A man, half Lothario, half Machiavelli, might usefully notice the excepted case.

Though I am a poor man, I would rather pay fifty pounds

than sit through any classical concert. It has been said that music is the food of love, but even for that I am too old.

If I should attempt to exhaust the list of incomparable Smiths who have enriched our national life, I should exhaust your patience.

Sir Edward Marshall-Hall once introduced me to an artist who undertook to paint my portrait for five hundred guineas. After many sittings a portrait was painted which no human witness has ever identified except the artist. It has been sent three times to Christie's. First it was described as an 'Italian Musician', and the highest bid was nine pounds. Next it was sent as a 'Medieval Poisoner', and fourteen pounds was the highest bid. Finally it was sent under the description 'A Non-Conformist Preacher'. A bid for seven pounds was hurriedly accepted; but, when the attempt was made to identify the bidder, it was found that he had disappeared.

I confess that I have never been of the number of those judges – I think indeed they are few – to whom the apprehension of being reversed on appeal causes serious alarm. I share with all my judicial colleagues under those circumstances the liberty of continuing to believe that they are right and the appellate court is wrong.

The profession of the bar is expressly precluded from advertising itself, but even there difficulties present themselves, because a learned counsel may not send his photograph in wig and gown to an illustrated newspaper but there is no law to prevent a photographer from sending it. It is extraordinary how enterprising our photographers are.

No one can pass an examination except people who have been working for two or three years in order to do so. It would be the most staggering performance ever known if the Archbishop of Canterbury could pass an examination in theology.

As for a Lord Chancellor who could pass the final examination for the bar, I do not believe that such a man has ever existed.

Is marriage with a step-mother to be permitted? I might perhaps suggest that the number of men ambitious of such a union will probably be limited.

My experience of general elections, which now goes back for nearly thirty years, has been that the moment an election is really concluded there is nobody in the country who does not give thanks that an experience at once so disagreeable, so costly and so fatiguing, is over.

A case in which F E Smith was employed came on for hearing late in the afternoon, and Mr Smith asked the judge to allow it to go over to the following day. 'I have been speaking all day in another court,' he said, 'and I am rather exhausted.' His request was granted. The clerk called the next case, and immediately a young counsel rose who, for some reason of his own, did not want the case to be tried at that time. He also requested that his case might be postponed. 'Why?' asked the judge coldly:

May it please you, my lord, I too, am in a state of exhaustion, for I have been listening all day to Mr Smith.

Votes are to swords exactly what banknotes are to gold – the one is effective only because the other is believed to be behind it.

* * *

Lord Birkett (1884–1962)

A discussion in the Court of Appeal in 1955 about the fact that a sufferer from double vision was wearing bifocal glasses:

But they are the commonest things in the world. I am wearing bifocals now, and in the old happy days they enabled one to look at the jury through the top half and look down at one's brief through the bottom half.

When addressing The English Association *on 'The Magic of Words' in 1953 he said:*

But you cannot spend long years in the law, as I have done, without being conscious that the lawyer for many of his purposes – his Statutes and Wills and Conveyances and the like – must resolutely eschew the words that have colour and content himself with the 'hereinbefores' and 'aforesaids' in order to achieve precision.

During his address to the Canadian Bar Association in 1947:

A friend of mine made application to postpone a case for three weeks. The judge, in assumed horror, said, 'But, Mr X, three weeks! Why, all the judges of the King's Bench Division might be dead by then.' To which my learned friend smilingly replied, 'Oh, my lord, that would be too much to hope for!'

* * *

Lord Brampton (1817–1907)

When Lord Brampton (then Mr Hawkins) was prosecuting counsel at the Tichborne trial, over which Chief Justice Cockburn pre-

sided, he was at one stage examining the antecedents of a man who had given sensational evidence for the claimant. In answer to a question, the witness said that he knew the man to be married, but that his wife passed under another name:

What name? *asked Mr Hawkins.*
Mrs Hawkins, *replied the witness.*
What was her maiden name? *continued Hawkins.*
Cockburn.
The coincidence produced long and hearty laughter.

It was once the duty of Mr H F Dickens, KC, son of the famous novelist, to examine before Mr Justice Hawkins a witness by the name of Pickwick. On the day on which the action was on the list, Mr Dickens was unable to attend, and, not wanting to miss the pleasure of seeing Dickens examine Pickwick, Mr Justice Hawkins adjourned the case. At last Mr Dickens was able to appear in court, the case was opened, and he called Mr Pickwick. 'I do not know, gentlemen', said Mr Dickens, addressing the jury, 'whether Mr Pickwick will appear in his gaiters':

When the eagerly-looked-for witness stepped into the box, it was generally declared that he was about the thinnest man ever seen in the courts.

Hawkins was sitting at the Lincoln Assize Court on the morning of the Lincoln Handicap. At the close of a case, he blandly addressed the jury as follows: 'Gentlemen of the jury, it has been brought to my notice that there is an event of some local importance about to take place this afternoon. I should be loth to stand for a moment between you and your participation in the celebration. Any expression of opinion on your part, therefore, will receive my most serious consideration.' The only desire of the jury, however, was to get the business of the court finished so that they could get back to their trades. So, after a few moments deliberation, the foreman arose and announced that they had 'no expression of opinion to offer':

I thank you for your communication, gentlemen. The court is adjourned until eleven o'clock tomorrow morning.

A barrister prosecuting, before Judge Hawkins, a man accused of stealing a teacup, had, in the middle of his address to the jury, a telegram placed in his hand. Instantly the impetuous recipient, who had taken a five-shilling chance in the bar 'sweep', exclaimed joyously: 'Silvio's won – and I've won.' His lordship, taken aback by this extraordinary proceeding, demanded to know the meaning of it. The barrister apologised profusely for his conduct, and begged forgiveness. Hawkins replied:

It is most improper, and I trust it will never occur again.

The barrister was just about to resume, when the judge intervened:

Oh, by the way, Mr —, did the telegram say what was second and third?

An old woman in the witness box had been rambling on in a voluble and incomprehensible manner. Mr Justice Hawkins, in order to clear the air, attempted a soothing question, but the old woman would not have it at any price. 'I have told you all I know,' she replied testily:

That may be, but the question rather is, do you know all that you have told us?

As a great sporting judge, Mr Justice Hawkins was particularly anxious to go to the Derby. Without revealing his desire he asked a certain QC, whose interests lay in quite another direction, to press for an adjournment of his case. Accordingly the QC, to oblige the judge, rose the next day and put the request. 'I am afraid, Mr —', said Hawkins in reply, 'that except for some good reason I cannot interfere with the ordinary course of business.' 'Well, m'lord, the fact is, it is a matter of very personal convenience.':

Oh well, of course in that case I have nothing further to say, and the case is adjourned. But I strongly suspect, Mr —, you want to go to a certain meeting – oh, you wicked old man!

It is told of Mr Justice Hawkins that a heavily marked brief in a compensation case was once delivered at his chambers, and that after six weeks had elapsed, and the hearing of the case was approaching, his clerk wrote to the solicitor suggesting that a cheque for the fee was not only desirable, but was in accordance with the usual practice of the profession. To this the solicitor replied:

If Mr Hawkins had taken the trouble to open the brief he would have found the cheque inside.

Soon after he had ascended the bench, Hawkins (once described as a 'racy and turf-attending judge') was hearing a murder trial. Counsel for the prosecution saw the prisoner say something to a constable, and demanded that what had been said should be disclosed. 'Yes,' said his lordship, 'I think you may demand that. Constable, inform the court what passed between you and the prisoner.' 'I – I would rather not, your lordship. I was . . . .' 'Never mind what you would rather not do. Inform the court what the prisoner said':

He asked me, your lordship, who that hoary heathen with the sheepskin was, as he had often seen him at the race-course.

* * *

Lord Brougham (1778–1868)

Lord Brougham tells a story of a case of assault and battery, where a stone was thrown by the defendant. The following evidence was drawn out of a Yorkshire man:

Did you see the defendant throw the stone?

I saw a stone, and I'm pretty sure the defendant throwed it.

Was it a large stone?

I should say it was a largish stone.

What was its size?

I should say a sizeable stone.

Can't you answer definitely how big it was?

I should say it was a stone of some bigness.

Can't you give the jury some idea of the stone?

Why, as near as I recollect, it wur something of a stone.

Can't you compare it to some other object?

Why, if I were to compare it, so as to give some notion of the stone, I should say it wur as large as a lump of chalk!

Lord Brougham had a great horror of hearing the interminable speeches of junior counsel. Once after listening to the speeches of two counsel on one side, from ten o'clock until half past two, a third rose to address the court on the same side. His lordship was quite unprepared for the additional infliction and exclaimed:

'What! Mr A, are you really going to speak on the same side?' 'Yes, my lord, I mean to trespass on your lordship's attention for a short time':

Then, then Mr A, you had better cut your speech as short as possible, otherwise you must not be surprised if you see me dozing; for really this is more than human nature can endure.

The position of Chief Baron of the Exchequer is said to have been offered to Brougham and refused on the ground that it would prevent his sitting in Parliament. 'True,' was the reply, 'but you will then be only one stage from the Woolsack.' Brougham replied:

Yes, but the horses will be off.

Defining a lawyer:

A legal gentleman who rescues your estate from your enemies, and keeps it himself.

* * *

Mr Justice Buckley (b 1906)

The principle of *noscitur a souis* does not in my judgment entitle one to overlook self-evident facts. If you meet seven men with black hair and one with red hair, you are not entitled to say that here are eight men with black hair.

It would normally be as impossible for a riparian owner to [use water for 'extraordinary' purposes] with absolutely no risk of wastage . . . as it would have been for Shylock to cut his pound of flesh without shedding any blood.

* * *

Lord Carson (1854–1935)

While appearing for the Crown in a divorce suit, defence counsel questioned a witness about the financial support he had received from the Crown. He had worn a new grey suit at the police court. Was he not now wearing a new blue one?:

LORD CARSON: Really, Mr Gill, we could not bring him unfrocked.

MR JUSTICE DARLING: If they had not dressed him he might have pawned the sheets.

LORD CARSON: The real terror, my lord, was that he might have pawned the new suit.

Lord Carson was arguing a case before three judges when Mr Justice Lawson, notorious for his sharp tongue, interrupted him. 'Mr Carson, you have no case.' Undeterred, Carson continued his speech. Some time later Lawson again interrupted him. 'Mr Carson, I say you have got no case.' Carson replied:

My lord, I heard you say that twenty minutes ago and knew it would be useless to argue the merits of the case with your lordship – I have been addressing the other judges!

Cross-examining a witness who was partial to alcohol:

LORD CARSON: Should I be right in calling you a heavy drinker?

WITNESS: That is my business.

LORD CARSON: Any other business?

PRESIDENT: I decline to hear you.

LORD CARSON: I must press this matter. I will ask for a vote to be taken to see if every commissioner takes your view.

PRESIDENT: I will not hear you further, and I will order you to withdraw.

LORD CARSON: I insist upon my right till every commissioner orders me to withdraw. I will stand up here and now for justice to be done.

PRESIDENT: The commissioners have consulted and we have come to the unanimous conclusion that we will not hear you. . . .

LORD CARSON: My lord, if I am not allowed to cross-examine I say the whole thing is a farce and a sham. I willingly withdraw from it. I will not prostitute my position by remaining longer as an advocate before an English judge.

PRESIDENT: I am not sitting as a judge.

LORD CARSON (*in a loud whisper*): Any fool can see that.

Upon becoming a Queen's Counsel he had, as was customary, to present himself to be called by each judge within the bar. In one court the business of the day was over and the formality could not be completed. In that court, the next morning, Mr Carson was engaged in a case. The judge, Mr Justice Kekewich, was a stickler for etiquette. As Carson began to address him, he remarked: 'Mr Carson, I cannot hear you.' Carson raised his voice. 'Mr Carson, I cannot hear you', the judge repeated. Carson regretted that his lordship was unable to hear a voice that had not previously been inaudible to the bench. 'Mr Carson,' said the judge, 'you do not take my point. You have not been called within the bar of my court. However, I will not send you home to put on your knee-

breeches.' At this Carson was heard to murmur, 'I should hope not.' 'What's that you say?' asked the judge, 'I warn you I shall tolerate no impertinence.' Carson replied:

I thought your lordship could not hear.

* * *

Mr Justice Cassels (b 1877)

When a witness under cross-examination in a slander action wanted to address a question to counsel, he directed:

No, no. This is only a one way traffic. We cannot have it turning into a roundabout.

He described the Probate, Divorce and Admiralty Division of the High Court:

Where the judges are perfectly at home, whether they are dealing with collisions at sea, or collisions on land, and provide every facility, so long as the estate is large enough, for relatives to display their extreme affection for each other when quarrelling over what has been left.

Comment on the Chancery Division of the High Court:

The place where the judges tell limited companies how they should deal with shareholders' money so that it won't be noticed.

Describing the House of Lords in its capacity as the 'top' court in the land:

Here you will find the most learned and most experienced of judges sitting in pre-war suits and delivering decisions which are absolutely final.

His comment on the bench:

A praiseworthy assembly of Englishmen – with a few Lancastrians and Yorkshiremen thrown in. . . .

He described the King's Bench Division of the High Court, of which he was a member, in the following way:

The finest division of all, the most distinguished and learned and illustrious. Every form of human frailty comes up before us – and gets it.

Of judges:

We are not really so bad as we look.

There might be evidence from which it might be reasonable to infer that he must have been in if he was seen coming out.

*   *   *

Mr Justice Cave (1832–1897)

In a fishery dispute before Mr Justice Cave, counsel representing one of the parties got up and read half a dozen original deeds of the reign of Elizabeth I. This was too much for Mr Justice Cave:

Now, the counsel for the owner of this fishery has proved a title of one hundred years. That is long enough for anyone. But you, his opponent, stand there and read out a lot of dusty, fusty old parchments of the reign of Queen Elizabeth, with what you say are different boundaries. You would uproot the title of every man in England if you had your way. I won't have it. There may be another world in which they will let you do it, but you shall not do it here!

*   *   *

Sir Arthur Channell (1838–1928)

When still Serjeant Channell, he was appearing for one side in a shipping case. He always had great difficulty in pronouncing his Hs, and during the trial he continually referred to the ship as the Ellen *while the opposing counsel, Sir Frederick Thesiger, called it the* Helen. *At last the judge in despair called 'Stop! What is the name of the ship? I have on my notes the* Helen, *and the* Ellen. *Which is it?' To which Thesiger replied in his blandest manner:*

Oh! my lord, the ship was christened the *Helen*, but she lost her 'H' in the chops of the Channell!

* * *

Lord Chapman (1803–1881)

Observation in Attwood v. Scott:

Experience is not sufficiently uniform to raise a presumption that one who has the means of paying a debt will actually pay it.

* * *

Mr Justice Chapman (b 1907)

In spite of, or perhaps because of, her red hair, she has, in my judgment, a head which is screwed on very firmly.

... I do not profess to be a stockbroker or merchant banker or a computer....

* * *

Lord Justice Chitty (1828–1899)

In a case before Lord Justice Chitty, counsel had been arguing for a considerable time about a bill of sale. 'I will now proceed to address myself to the furniture – an item covered by the bill', counsel continued. Whereupon the weary judge commented:

You have been doing nothing else for the last hour.

* * *

Lord Clare (1749–1802)

One day, when it was known that a certain barrister called Curran was to make an elaborate argument in Chancery, Lord Clare brought a large Newfoundland dog upon the bench with him, and during the progress of the argument, lent his ear much more to the dog than to the barrister. At last the Chancellor turned aside, in the most material part of the argument, and began, in full court, to fondle the animal. Curran stopped short. 'Go on, go on, Mr Curran,' cried Lord Clare:

Oh! I beg a thousand pardons, my lord, I really took it for granted that your lordship was employed in consultation.

* * *

Lord Clayton (1702–1770)

Chief Justice Clayton, of the King's Bench in Ireland, was an Englishman. One day he said to a Mr Harwood, a learned and witty Irish barrister, that 'numerous as were the English laws, one was found to be the key to the other; whereas here it is just the contrary, as your laws are so continually clashing, that upon my word, at times I don't clearly understand them'.

Very true, indeed, my lord, that is what we all say.

* * *

Lord Coleridge (1821–1893)

When at the bar, Coleridge was counsel in a case in which an Irish lady was suing the superior of a religious order for expulsion without reasonable cause. Coleridge cross-examined a Mrs Kennedy, one of the superintendents of the convent, who mentioned in her evidence that the plaintiff had been found in the pantry eating strawberrys when she should have been attending class duties:

MR COLERIDGE: Eating strawberries, really!

MRS KENNEDY: It was forbidden, sir.

MR COLERIDGE: And did you, Mrs Kennedy, really consider there was any harm in that?

MRS KENNEDY: No, sir, not in itself, any more than there was in eating an apple; but you know, sir, the mischief that came from that.

When a young man at the bar, he had a small case on the Western Circuit before Baron Martin, who was rough in manner, though kind of heart. During the course of an elaborate and eloquent defence, his lordship interrupted rather sharply. Coleridge, with great dignity, said that if he were again interrupted he would have to retire from the case. 'Why?' asked his lordship. 'Because', replied Coleridge with even more dignity, 'it is obvious that my client will suffer, since I am not so fortunate as to win your lordship's favour':

Oh! go on, go on, I think you are a very respectable young man!

* * *

Lord Coleridge (1851–1921)

When, as Lord Chief Justice, Coleridge was visiting the United States, he was continually pestered by interviewers, one of whom, failing to draw him, began to disparage Britain. Lord Coleridge bore it all in good part. Finally the interviewer said, 'I am told, my lord, you think a great deal of your Great Fire of London. Well, I say that the conflagration we had in Chicago made your Great Fire look very small.' To which his lordship blandly responded:

Sir, I have every reason to believe that the Great Fire of London was quite as great as the people of that time desired.

* * *

Mr Justice Coleridge (1790–1876)

In Thimblerig v Hookey:

This action was brought to recover damages for having been called a villain and the plaintiff alleges, somewhat boldly as I think, that on that account his friends have deserted him. But I hope I may be allowed to say that, in my humble opinion, such of his acquaintance as I had the advantage of seeing when they came as witnesses at the trial, would rather cease to associate with the plaintiff if they thought he did not deserve the title the defendent had bestowed upon him than if they believed he did; and besides, I think – I speak for myself – I think it can be no loss to any man, but rather a distinct gain, to be deprived of the consort of such friends as the plaintiff appears to have been – ahem – blessed with.

As to the term villain or villein – for it is nowhere shown which spelling the defendant intended – let us consider whether, as applied to the plaintiff, it is a defamatory word or not.

A villein, if I have not forgotten my Oxford learning, was one who did odd jobs. A villein carried food to the pigs – but the plaintiff is a tout, and supplies sporting intelligence. The villein was dependent on a lord, and was his 'man' – *Homo sum: humani nihil a me alienum puto*; but as to what I think of the plaintiff – well I *say* nothing.

* * *

John Curran (1750–1817)

Soon after being called to the bar, he observed of a statement of Judge Robinson's, the author of scurrilous political pamphlets, that he had never met the law, as laid down by his lordship, **in** *any book in his library:*

JUDGE: That may be, sir, but I suspect that your library is very small.

CURRAN: I find it more instructive, my lord, to study good works than to compose bad ones. My books may be few, but the title pages give me the writers' names, and my shelf is not disgraced by any such rank absurdities, that their very own authors are shamed to own them.

JUDGE: Sir, you are forgetting the respect which you owe to the dignity of the judicial character.

CURRAN: Dignity! my lord, upon that point I shall cite you a case . . . So my lord, when the person entrusted with the dignity of the judgment seat lays it aside for a moment to enter into a disgraceful personal contest, it is in vain when he has been worsted in the encounter that he seeks to resume it – it is in vain that he tries to shelter himself behind an authority which he has abandoned.

JUDGE: If you say another word I shall commit you.

CURRAN: If your lordship shall do so, we shall both of us have the consolation of reflecting, that I am not the worst thing your lordship has committed.

*   *   *

Lord Darling (1849–1936)

In a turf libel case, Justice Darling at one point intervened to comment on the statement made by a witness, that a horse is made fit by running on the course before he is expected to win a race, and added: 'That is so, not only on the race course. You can never make a good lawyer by putting him to read in the library.' To which the defendant, who was conducting his own case, replied: 'But I take it a barrister does try'. Responded Darling:

You have no notion how he tries the judge.

In another turf libel case, a question arose as to whether the stewards of the Jockey Club had the power to check riding 'short', and the judge inquired if the stewards could say, 'You must ride with a leather of a prescribed length'. He got the answer, 'Yes; they could say if you don't ride longer we won't give you a licence'. Darling replied:

Which means if you don't ride longer you won't ride long.

In a case in which defending counsel asked for three months' adjournment in order to get a translation of some technical German documents necessary to his case, Darling said, 'I can understand that you should apply for some delay, but why three months?'

Counsel replied, 'The plaintiff's documents which require translation are so technical,' whereupon Darling commented:

Rather a good idea has occurred to me. Why not go to someone who knows German already?

When complimented at a Press Club dinner on his great knowledge of Latin and Greek. He replied:

I am afraid I never learned Greek and know nothing of the language. All I remember reading about the Greeks was that they sent out a number of ships the majority of which were wrecked. (*A pause*) As far as I can understand from reading the Law Reports they've been doing the same thing ever since.

A counsel was trying to discredit a witness, and asked him: 'Are you a married man?' 'I am,' said the witness. 'How many children have you got?' 'Two,' replied the witness. After putting a few more questions, counsel again said significantly: 'You have two children, you say, and you are married?' At this point Mr Justice Darling interpolated:

He told you he had two children a few moments ago: there are hardly likely to have been any fresh arrivals since your first question!

In an action the issue was whether the plaintiff, who had been engaged by the defendant to sing in 'potted opera' at a music hall, was competent to fulfil his contract. 'Well, he could not sing like the archangel Gabriel,' a witness said, in reply to the plaintiff's counsel. 'I have never heard the archangel Gabriel,' commented the eminent KC. Darling's swift rejoinder was:

Well, that is a pleasure yet to come.

He said of Sir Edward Carson, when the latter was being attacked for his final speech as prosecutor in an action concerning the validity of a divorce:

The main part of the objection seems to be that the Solicitor General is eloquent. I cannot interfere in the exercise by the Solicitor General of a natural gift.

While trying a man for disturbing a service at St Paul's Cathedral, counsel submitted that any interruption of a church service came under the legal definition of brawling. To which Judge Darling replied:

Is it not putting it rather high? Take, for instance, a quite impossible case; suppose someone were to say 'Encore' at the end of the sermon?

He dealt with a certain witness who said that he had been wedded to the truth from infancy by asking him how long he had been a widower.

He described his thoughts during a trial in a court which was not his own, while he was sitting beside the presiding judge:

I looked at the accused as sentence was passed upon him and saw his hand go in the direction of his pocket. I was horrified. Good heavens! I thought, he has got a gun and is going to have a shot at Bigham [the judge]. These people are always too strung up to aim straight, and he is bound to miss Bigham and hit me. What a way to end my judicial career – shot, and not even in my own court!

The following took place during the cross-examination of a music master:

COUNSEL: I want someone upon whom you could have relied as showing you could produce the perfect singing voice.

PLAINTIFF: I had meant those whose voices were perfectly produced; the pupils were satisfied.

MR JUSTICE DARLING: Many people are satisfied with themselves who cannot satisfy others.

PLAINTIFF: I give people the full compass of which they are capable. If they have no ear, they cannot sing.

MR JUSTICE DARLING: Any of the persons taught by your correspondence system might never be able to sing?

PLAINTIFF: Yes.

MR JUSTICE DARLING: But he would be satisfied with his own performance?

PLAINTIFF: Yes.

MR JUSTICE DARLING: As I understand it, if his system were applied to a crow and a canary, one would be the perfect singing crow and the other the perfect singing canary!

Disposing of a colourful address delivered before him in a certain case by Marshall Hall, he said to the jury:

Mr Marshall Hall has been addressing you on the snakes in the road and the snakes in the grass. I do not know if it has been of any assistance to you to come to a decision in this matter, but it has not helped me in the slightest, and since the subject matter under discussion is a nautical one, his simile might at least have referred to sea serpents!

MR JUSTICE DARLING: It used to be said that the common law of England resided in the breasts of His Majesty's judges.

COUNSEL: A very happy residence.

MR JUSTICE DARLING: This does not justify what are called exploratory operations.

In a case stated from the Magistrates' Courts by Horatio Bottomley:

I suppose you would not have denied it if you had been accused of writing *Paradise Lost.*

HORATIO BOTTOMLEY: Yes, I should, I've written much better verses than that.

* * *

Lord Davey (1833–1907)

LORD MANSFIELD: If this be law, sir, I must burn all my books, I see.

SERJEANT DAVY: Your lordship had better read them first.

* * *

Mr Justice Davies (b 1913)

When a witness in a probate action in 1955 said that the testator was lugubrious and had no sense of humour, he is reported to have observed:

Rather like some judges!

* * *

Mr Justice Day (1826–1908)

At the Leeds Assizes a witness in a case deposed that the defendant spoke of the plaintiff as a 'damned thief'. The defendant's counsel at once interposed in correction: 'A damned thief of a lawyer, my lord.' Justice Day:

That addition renders the saying perfectly innocuous.

When at the bar, Mr Justice Day had a great tendency to urge his clients to compromise, which earned him the appropriate title of 'settling day'.

* * *

Thomas Day (1748–1789)

Thomas Day had Sir William Jones as a fellow student in the Middle Temple. One day they were taking down an old book when a large, black spider was dislodged and fell on the floor. 'Day,' cried Jones, 'kill that spider.' Day replied:

No, I will not kill that spider. I do not know that I have a right to kill it. Suppose when you were going on your walk to Westminster Hall a superior being who perhaps may have as much power over you as you have over that spider should say to his companion 'Kill that lawyer!' how should you like that, Jones? And I am sure to most people a lawyer is a more noxious animal than a spider.

*　*　*

Lord Denning (b 1899)

Commenting on the Land Compensation Act (1961):

I must say that rarely have I come across such a mass of obscurity, even in a statute. I cannot conceive how any ordinary person can be expected to understand it. So deep is the thicket that before the Lands Tribunal both of the very experienced counsel lost their way.

What is the argument on the other side? Only this, that no case has been found in which it has been done before.

That argument does not appeal to me in the least. If we never do anything which has not been done before, we shall never get anywhere. The law will stand still whilst the rest of the world goes on; and that will be bad for both.

I would allow this appeal and give judgment for the moneylender. I have set out the mathematics in an appendix – it is not fit to read aloud or at all.

What matters in England is that each man should be free to develop his own personality to the full: and the only duties which should restrict this freedom are those which are necessary to enable everyone else to do the same. Whenever these interests are nicely balanced, the scale goes down on the side of freedom.

*   *   *

Lord Dilhorne (b 1905)

On the undesirability of appointments to the bench for political reasons, he said:

I remember two magistrates' courts when I was a young barrister, one staffed by members of one political party, the other by members of another political party. There was nothing to choose between them. They enjoyed an equally bad reputation!

*   *   *

Lord Justice Diplock (b 1907)

I find it almost impossible to accept that, in these egalitarian and materialistic days, the feelings and pride of a reasonable man are more affronted if his wife commits adultery with an opulent baronet rather than with an impoverished dustman, with a young Adonis rather than an elderly Caliban. The lower the material and physical attractions of his supplanter, the more wounding the comparison, and the greater the blow to his own self esteem.

The measure of the second element of damages (for adultery), compensation for injury to the husband's feelings and pride, must also take account of changing social norms. The rest must be his rational resentment, not his mere idiosyncratic ire, and the factors to be taken into account in mitigation or aggravation are those which would affect the feelings of a reasonable man with an unfaithful wife in the social condition of today. Such reasonable cuckold of the common law may be divorced from reality as well as from his wife, but the concept is needed. . . .

Thomas William Harkness, retired boiler lagger, if he had followed, as I have no doubt he has, the intricacies of the interlocutory proceedings in this case, must have thought that 'the law is an ass'. I am not sure that this judgment will change his opinion, but at any rate he will not feel it is such an unjust ass as he must have felt before.

But however anomalous it may be, the rule of public policy, that the court will not enforce a 'penalty clause', so as to permit a party to a contract to recover in an action a sum greater than the measure of damages to which he would be entitled at common law, is well established, and in these days when so often one party cannot satisfy his contractual hunger *à la carte* but only at the *table d'hôte* of a standard printed contract, it has certainly not outlived its usefulness.

There is no room today for mystique in the law of negligence. It is the application of common morality and common sense to the activities of the common man.

It would be a poor compliment to the draftsman of this section of the Tenancy Act, 1960, if this court were to be unanimous as to its meaning.

When sitting with his learned brethren, Lord Justices Harman and Russell, he agreed with their judgments on appeal 'with that humility becoming to a common lawyer when confronted with such an archaic branch of the Chancery Law'.

* * *

Sir Gerald Dodson (1884–1967)

Addressing a wife charged with administering a noxious substance to her husband, Sir Gerald commented:

Husbands no doubt have their defects, but these are not to be remedied by giving them doses of disinfectant.

Summing up for the jury:

This is the third case running of this kind that I have tried. It almost leads one to believe that if there is one dangerous place on the cross-roads, it is a pedestrian crossing.

* * *

Lord Eldon (1751–1838)

I remember, in one case where I was counsel, for a long time the evidence did not appear to touch the prisoner at all, and he looked about him with the most perfect unconcern seeming to think himself quite safe. At last the surgeon was called, who stated deceased had been killed by a shot, a gunshot in the head; and he produced the matted hair and stuff cut from and taken out of the wound. It was all hardened with blood. A basin of warm water was brought into court, and as the blood was gradually softened, a piece of printed paper appeared, the wadding of the gun, which proved to be the half of a ballad. The other half had been found in the man's pocket when he was taken. He was hanged.

To illustrate unreasonable complaints against public functionaries Lord Eldon would relate that on the circuit, stopping at a place where many years before a friend had been curate, he had the curiosity to ask the landlord of the inn whether he remembered him. 'Yes,' answered he with an oath, 'I well remember him. I have had reason enough to remember him. It was the worst day this parish ever saw that brought him here.' The lawyer afraid of hearing something hard said, 'Mr Moises, I am certain, was a respectable man.' 'That may be,' cried the landlord, 'but he married me to the worst wife that ever man was plagued with.' 'Oh! is that all? That was your own fault; she was your own choice not Mr Moises'.' :

Yes, but I could not have married her if there had not been a parson to marry us.

While Sir Thomas Davenport, a very dull orator, was making a long speech at the York Assizes, a chimney sweep boy, who had climbed up to a dangerous place in front of a high gallery, having been put to sleep by him, fell down and was killed. Whereupon I being then Attorney General of the circuit indicted Sir Thomas in our Grand Court for the murder of the boy; and the indictment (according to the rule of law which requires that the weapon shall be described, and that there shall be an averment of its value or that it is of no value) alleged that the murder was committed with a 'certain blunt instrument of no value called a "long speech".'

Lord Eldon is said to have given this account of a trial at York arising out of a horse race:

One of the conditions was that each horse should be ridden by a gentleman. In an action for the stakes the question arose 'whether the plaintiff was a gentleman or not'. After much evidence and oratory on both sides the judge thus summed up:

'Gentlemen of the jury, when I see you in that box I call you gentlemen, for I know you are such there; but out of that box I do not know what may be the requisites that constitute a gentleman; therefore I can give you no direction except that you will consider your verdict.'

The jury found for the defendant.

Next morning the plaintiff challenged both Law and me, who were conducting the case against him; for having said he was no gentleman. We sent him this answer, 'that we could not think of fighting one who had been found no gentleman by the solemn verdict of twelve of his countrymen'.

I remember Mr Justice Gould trying a case at York, and when he had proceeded for about two hours, he observed 'Here are only eleven jurymen; where is the twelfth?'

'Please you, my lord,' said one of the eleven, 'he is gone away about some business, but he has left his verdict with me.'

The following story is told by Lord Eldon of Serjeant Davy and Serjeant Whitaker:

SERJEANT DAVY: Brother Whitaker, how unfortunate we have been in not insuring those pipes of Madeira! The vessel on board of which they were is lost, and our Madeira is at the bottom of the sea, and now you and I have to pay our money for nothing.

SERJEANT WHITAKER: Our Madeira! I don't know what you mean. I have nothing to do with any Madeira.

SERJEANT DAVY: What! You surely don't mean to deny that we were to be joint purchasers of two pipes, which, for improvement, were to go to the East Indies and back, and now to get off paying your half of what we jointly purchased.

SERJEANT WHITAKER: I never entered into such an arrangement.

SERJEANT DAVY: Well, then, I am glad of it. It is the finest Madeira that ever came into the Thames. The ship and wine are safe, and the wine is all my own.

Sir James Graham, the solicitor, was at one time engaged in a great many private and other bills, and was frequently entrusted with the office of carrying the bills from the Lower to the Upper House. One evening Sir James came to the bar no less than twelve times, with twelve separate bills. Twelve times was the Chancellor, Lord Eldon, compelled to come down to the bar, purse in hand, to receive them. On the twelfth time Lord Eldon said to the solicitor:

What, have you got another? When I used to know you first you used to be called James Graham, but now we'll call you Bill Graham.

During the trials of Hardy, Horne Took and Thelwall in 1794, in concluding his speech against Horne Took, Attorney General Scott (later Lord Eldon) cried: 'It is the little inheritance I have to leave to my children, and by God's help, I will leave it unimpaired.' Here he shed tears; and to the astonishment of the court the Solicitor General (Mitford) began to weep in court. 'Just look at Mitford,' said a bystander to Horne Took, 'what on earth is he crying for?' :

He is crying to think of the *little* inheritance Scott's children are likely to get.

Lord Eldon in Campbell v Stein :

It is with great regret, if that expression may properly come from a judicial mouth, that I am compelled to say that this action cannot be maintained.

Mr Solicitor General may remember a case in which he was concerned before me, where the gentlemen on both sides went into a lengthened discussion, communicated most detailed information, and had actually brought the case to a very extreme stage, and yet had never made the slightest mention of an act of parliament most vitally affecting the ultimate decision or the question : nor would it ever have been mentioned had I not been so fortunate as to know it.

Jogeph Hume once described Lord Eldon's Chancellorship as 'the sreatest curse which fell on any nation was to have such a Chancellor and such a Court of Chancery'. Lord Eldon wrote of this attack in a letter to his grandson Lord Encombe:

You see Mr Hume called your grandfather 'a curse to the country'. He dignified also the quietest, meekest man in the country with the title of a 'firebrand', ie the Bishop of London. I met the Bishop at the Exhibition, and as it happened to be an uncommonly cold day, in this most unusually cold weather, I told him that the curse of the country was so very cold that I hoped he would allow him to keep himself warm by sitting next to the firebrand; and so we laughed and amused ourselves with this fellow's impertinence.

A plaintiff, Metcalfe, had a patent for hair-brushes of a particular sort, and the defendant Thompson was selling brushes of the same sort without licence. No counsel at first appeared for the defendant. Lord Chancellor Eldon said:

This injunction must be brushed off, unless some counsel be here to support it.

* * *

Lord Ellenborough (1790–1871)

Lord Ellenborough objected to interruptions in court, and used to be greatly annoyed during the season of colds by the noise of coughing. On one such occasion, he took the opportunity of a slight cessation to remark in his usual emphatic manner:

Some slight interruption one might tolerate, but there seems to be an industry of coughing.

He once complained about the appearance of a witness, a bricklayer by profession, who came to be sworn. 'Really, witness, when you have to appear before this court, it is your bounden duty to be more clean and decent in your appearance.' 'Upon my life,' replied the witness, 'if your lordship come to that, I am every bit as well dressed as your lordship.' 'How do you mean, sir?':

Why, faith, you come here in your working clothes and I come in mine.

An eminent conveyancer when giving a long harangue had effectively cleared the court and appeared insensible to the yawning impatience of the ushers. The clock struck four, and the judges started to their feet. The barrister appealed to know when it would be their lordships' pleasure to hear the remainder of his argument. Lord Ellenborough replied:

Mr P, we are bound to hear you, and shall do so on Friday, but pleasure has long been out of the question.

* * *

Lord Tinwald (1680–1763)

Erskine (later Lord Tinwald) and a Dr Parr were fond of bandying words with each other. Parr one day told Erskine that, if he survived him, he would write his epitaph. Erskine replied:

You are wrong to say that, doctor, for you hold out to me an inducement to commit suicide.

Erskine was talking in court one day with a Mr Lamb, when Erskine remarked how much the practice of speaking gave a man confidence in addressing the court. 'I protest I don't find it so,' said Mr Lamb, 'for though I've been a good many years at the bar, and have had my share of business, I don't find my confidence increases; indeed, the contrary is rather my case.' To which Erskine replied:

Why, it's nothing unusual that a lamb should grow sheepish!

Couplet by Erskine on Mr Justice Ashurst:

Judge Ashurst with his lanthorn jaws
Throws light upon the English laws.

* * *

Lord Evershed (1899–1966)

Mr Justice Evershed remarked during a case concerning the registration of a word as a trademark for footwear:

It is necessary . . . that I should, first, say something of the word which has been the subject matter of the argument. It is 'comphies'. In speaking of it as a word, as one must, one is, I think, paying it a compliment, because it barely deserves such an appellation which makes it part of articulate speech, which is said by some to be the only distinguishing feature between the human race and brute beasts. . . .

Without attempting further analysis, when all the circumstances of the origin and the novelty of the word 'comphies' are considered, I do not think that it can properly and justly be said that 'comphies', applied to footwear, has a direct reference to the character or quality of that footwear. Not having such a direct reference and not being a geographical name (so far as I know), and, I hope, not being a surname . . . the applicants are entitled to succeed.

* * *

Serjeant Fazakerley (d 1767)

Serjeant Fazakerley was 'pumped' for information one day while riding out with a rich squire who had a lawsuit pending. The serjeant gave his opinion in such a way the squire was encouraged to proceed with the lawsuit – but after spending much money he lost his suit. Irritated and disappointed, he visited the serjeant at his chambers and exclaimed: 'Mr Serjeant, here I have lost three thousand pounds by your advice.' 'By my advice,' replied Fazakerley, 'how can that be? I don't remember giving you my advice, but let me look over my book': 'Book, there is no occasion to look at your books; it was when we were riding out together':

Oh! I remember something of it; but that was only my travelling opinion, and my opinion is never to be relied on, except it is registered in my fee-book.

* * *

Mr Justice Gerrard (b 1903)

Describing the corridors and passages of the Law Courts, when, early in January 1954, he sat in a converted room on the third floor:

To get here I have been up the rocky mountains and down in the leafy glen. I was completely out of breath.

* * *

Lord Goddard (b 1877)

It is recorded that Blackstone always wrote with a bottle of port at his elbow? I had considered that myself, in writing a judgment, but concluded it would spoil the port.

* * *

Mr Justice Graham (1744–1836)

Justice Graham was known as a polite judge and in his final speech to a burglar once said:

My honest friend, you are found guilty of a felony, for which it is my painful duty to . . .

* * *

Mr Justice Grantham (1835–1911)

On one occasion, when he was judge at the Newcastle Assizes, Mr Justice Grantham left the house where he was staying, one night, to post his letters. As he was wearing a cap, he was not recognised by police the officer who was on duty outside, and the constable inquired of his lordship if the old — had gone to bed yet. The judge replied that he thought not, and went on to post his letters. A short time later, he returned to the house, opened the bedroom window, and putting his head out, called:

Officer, the old — is just going to bed now!

* * *

Lord Greene (1883–1952)

The statement that time is infinitely divisible was said to be a scientific fact. I should prefer to call it a metaphysical conception. No doubt, when a bevy of angels is performing saltatory exercises on the point of a needle it is always possible to find room for one more, but propositions of this character appear to me to be ill suited for adoption by the law of this character which proceeds on principles of practical common sense.

A judge who observes the demeanour of the witnesses while they are being examined by counsel has from his detached position a much more favourable opportunity of forming a just appreciation than a judge who himself con-

(Left) Edward Carson, first Baron Carson (1854–1935)

(Below) Viscount Simonds, Lord High Chancellor of Great Britain 1951–4 (1881–)

(Above) The Hon. Sir Travers Humphreys (1867–1956)

(Right) Baron Brougham and Vaux (1778–1868)

(Right) Edward Thurlow, first Baron Thurlow (1731–1806)

(Below) Sir Frank Lockwood, Solicitor-General (1846–1897)

(Above) Frederick Smith, first Earl of Birkenhead (1872–1930)

(Right) The Hon. Henry Erskine (1746–1817)

ducts the examination. If he takes the latter course he, so to speak, descends into the arena and is liable to have his vision clouded by the dust of the conflict.

* * *

Sir Edward Marshall Hall (1858–1927)

Even as a young man he was not one to be silenced by a reproof from the bench. 'Sit down,' commanded one judge whom he had offended:

Certainly, my lord. If your lordship would prefer me to address you sitting down, I will do so.

In his defence of Robert Wood for the Camden Town murder, Sir Edward had to cross-examine a witness on his description of the defendant:

SIR EDWARD: Did you describe the man as of stiff build with broad shoulders?

WITNESS: Yes.

SIR EDWARD: Wood, stand up!

The accused rose, a slight figure with narrow shoulders.

SIR EDWARD: Now, do you describe that man as broad shouldered?

WITNESS: He looked broader with his overcoat on.

SIR EDWARD: Then he shall wear it.

Still Wood looked a slim figure.

SIR EDWARD: Would you describe that man as broad shouldered?

WITNESS: He has broader shoulders than I have.

SIR EDWARD: Would you call a bluebottle an elephant because it is bigger than a fly?

Sir Edward was often indefatigable in his interventions, offering every objection to the prosecution proceedings that his ingenuity could suggest. 'My lord,' he said during one case, 'I object.' 'That,' commented his lordship tartly, 'we can see for ourselves.' After a sustained argument he asked for the judge's indulgence. 'I hope, my lord, you will be patient with me.' To which his lordship rejoined:

I do not think you have any reason to complain about that.

* * *

Lord Halsbury (1823–1921)

When leader of the Welsh circuit, Lord Halsbury (Hardinge Giffard) appeared for a public body and devoted himself with more than usual energy to the interests of his clients. The presiding judge noticed this and remarked on it: 'You are not a Welshman, you know.' 'That is so,' assented Hardinge Giffard, 'but I have had a good deal out of Welshmen in my time':

Oh, I see. You are a Welshman by extraction!

* * *

Lord Hannen (1821–1890)

Mr Justice Hannen was known as a very strict and stern ruler of his court, and only on one occasion was a man ever known to take a liberty with him. A juryman, dressed in deep mourning, serious and downcast in expression, stood up and claimed exemption from service on that day, as he was deeply interested in the funeral of a gentleman at which it was his desire to be present. 'Oh certainly,' was the courteous reply of the judge, and the man left the court. 'My lord,' interposed the associate, as soon as the ex-juryman had gone, 'do you know who that man is whom you exempted?' 'No':

He is an undertaker.

* * *

Mr Justice Hardinge (1743–1816)

Mr Justice Hardinge addressing a grand jury at Cardiff:

I cannot forbear to admire the eloquence of the gaoler and of his calendar. There I perceive three little words, not to be surpassed by Demosthenes himself – 'None for trial.' May those brilliant words record and perpetuate the honour of this country for ages to come!

* * *

Lord Justice Harman (b 1894)

I cannot find any clear decision that the public has the right to walk on the foreshore when the tide is out, nor of landing from boats or embarking except in cases of emergency. It seems also clear enough that there is no public highway along the foreshore. It is, on the other hand, notorious that in many and indeed in most places the use of the foreshore by the public for purposes of recreation and bathing is tolerated.

Accountants are the witch doctors of the modern world, and they too are apt to deal in unrealities. . . .

During a case on compulsory purchase:

This appeal is concerned with injurious affection, a piece of jargon having a respectable pedigree and prolific of litigation in our courts for a century or more, but none the better, I think, when embellished with the epithet which it acquired during the hearing when it was styled 'pure injurious affection'. It is not emotion but an effect which is being described.

In a case concerned with the rival claims of two fighters to use the title welterweight champion of Trinidad:

It occurred to me for the first time during the hearing to regret the desuetude of ordeal by battle as a method of trial.

Charity, we are taught, covers a multitude of sins, but whether that doctrine ought to extend to the draftsman of these documents may, I think, well be doubled.

* * *

C P Harvey (b 1900)

Commenting upon the fact that judges know no compulsory retiring age but receive a pension of £3,600 on voluntary retirement:

If the Knights of the Round Table could be resurrected in the present age and were all called to the bar, one can fancy them pursuing a vision of the Consolidated Fund with all the zest which they formerly directed to the Holy Grail.

* * *

Sir Patrick Hastings (1880–1952)

Cross-examining a witness with great severity: 'I advise you to answer the questions. The dramatic answer rang out:

The last time I took your advice I did twelve months.

* * *

Mr Justice Hilbery (b 1883)

COUNSEL: Mr Gardiner says that to err is only human . . .
MR JUSTICE HILBERY: Having regard to the existence of the Court of Appeal, I should think to err is also judicial.

* * *

Lord Hodson (b 1895)

In the Court of Appeal to a barrister who was whispering to a solicitor while another barrister was addressing the court:

I suffer from acute hearing; I can hear every word you say from up here.

* * *

Lord Huddleston (1815–1891)

Described a barrister's life as consisting of three stages:

In the first he is ambitious and cares only for work; in the second he is mercenary and cares only for fees; in the third, a stage reached only by a few, he cares neither for the work nor the fees.

* * *

Sir Travers Humphreys (1867–1956)

On being handed the customary pair of white gloves for a clean calendar:

I understand that early this morning a person attempted to qualify for attendance at these Assizes by breaking into the Huntingdon police station. However, so long as would-be criminals confine themselves to breaking into police stations the public can sleep in comfort.

The punishment for misconduct in this country is not death but the divorce court – though maybe this is becoming less and less of a punishment.

At an Assize Court enquiring whether the architect who designed the building was still alive:

Because if he is, I should like to exercise the powers I have of ordering his immediate execution. The witness box is carefully placed to make it as unlikely as possible that the jury should hear a single word that is said!

Complaining of the draught in his court at Winchester, when he was seventy, he sent for the county architect, and, placing him in the witness box, ordered him to attend to the draught as 'my right hand is so cold I can hardly write'. If the court were not made habitable by the following day, he threatened he would adjourn the Assize to Southampton. In a leader The Times *expressed approval of a judge who did not suffer draughts gladly:*

The law should always be administered in cold blood, so long as it is not too cold.

While trying a case in which a man of twenty-one was charged with an offence against a girl of fifteen, he reminded the jury that Parliament had decided that if a man were twenty-three or under he could offer the defence that he thought the girl concerned was over sixteen . . . :

Why a man of thirty or forty or fifty should be presumed to be a better judge of the age of a woman than a man of twenty-one, twenty-two, twenty-three or even nineteen, I do not think anyone has been able to understand. The Common Law is founded on common sense and is the glory of this country. The other law is made by politicians.

Commenting upon the book The Great Pearl Robbery *written by his son, Christmas Humphreys:*

I can only say that I have not discovered any misstatement of fact in it, while, as to the law, it is notorious that learned counsel know much more about this subject than any mere judge!

At the Old Bailey:

I am afraid it is a well known fact that the Government will pay higher prices for things than a private individual. Perhaps it is because they are buying with other people's money.

Upon hearing a police witness describe a road that 'staggered' near a public house:

I can quite understand that people who come out of a public house stagger, but I can't see how a road can stagger Do you mean it curves? Everything seems to stagger these days. Holidays are staggered; daylight is staggered; working-hours are staggered, and now roads are being staggered.

Upon being asked by the Royal Commission on Capital Punishment if he was in favour of hanging women:

Oh dear, yes! I am not in favour of making any difference between the sexes.

Upon placing a man on probation:

I cannot tell you to go away and live comfortably because I do not think anyone in this country is living comfortably at the present time.

*　　*　　*

William Hunnis (16th century)

Will of William Hunnis, a gentleman of the chapel to Edward VI, afterwards Chapel Master to Elizabeth I:

To God my soule I do bequeathe,
　because it is his owen,
My body to be layd in grave, where
　to my friends best knowen;
Executors I will none make, thereby
　great stryfe may grow,
Because the goods that I shall
　leave wyll not pay all I owe.

*　　*　　*

Lord Jenkins (b 1899)

The circumstances suggest that the plaintiffs are willing to wound and yet afraid to strike.

* * *

Earl Jowitt (1885–1957)

A lady handed a writ to her solicitor with the remark: 'It has come at last and they have a witness.' On being asked how she knew this she replied:

The name of the witness is on the writ. It must be the foreman on the job. I knew they called him William but I did not know his other name was Jowitt. He is the one who wasted a lot of time on the job and then has the cheek to put himself down as witness.

* * *

Lord Kenyon (1732–1802)

The case of Salkeld does not come very strongly recommended. For first, it is an anonymous case; and next, what is relied upon as there said was beside the point in judgment.

* * *

Lord Lee (1868–1947)

An erroneous reference to 'the late Lord Lee' by a correspondent in a letter to the Daily Telegraph *drew the reply from his lordship:*

May I plead that although, since my retirement, I have done my best to keep out of the newspapers (including the obituary columns) I am still reasonably alive and even liable to kick whenever sufficient provocation presents itself.

* * *

Sir Frank Lockwood (1847–1897)

Cross-examining the director of a rather doubtful company, who was giving evidence on its somewhat shady history, Lockwood asked him: 'Now sir, when did you first determine to float this company?' 'Float this company?' asked the witness, 'I don't know what you mean by "floating the company"':

Very well then, I will make myself perfectly clear. By 'floating' the company, I mean that operation which almost invariably precedes the 'sinking' of it. Do you understand me now?

Sir Frank Lockwood's first brief was on a petition to the Master of the Rolls for payment out of court of a sum of money. He appeared for the official liquidator of a company whose consent had to be obtained before the court would part with the fund. Lockwood was instructed to consent, for a fee of three guineas on the brief, and one guinea for consultation. The petition had been abundantly clear to the judge by counsel for the petitioner and counsel for the principal respondent. Then up rose Lockwood, and indicated his appearance in the case. 'What brings YOU *here?' asked the judge, wanting to know his function in the case. Lockwood looked puzzled. 'What do you come here for?' repeated the judge. The answer came back swiftly and triumphantly, after a quick glance at the front of the brief:*

Three and one, my lord!

Defending the murderer Charles Peace before Mr Justice Lopes, he was congratulated on his defence of Peace. He accepted the compliment, but added that:

It was not Peace at any price – because his pleading had been unfee'd.

Defending a man at York on a charge of stealing cattle – or 'beasts' as they were sometimes called locally, he said to the witness: 'Now my man, you say you saw X the defendant – how far can you see a beast to know it?':

Just as far off as I am from you.

* * *

Lord Lyndhurst (1772–1863)

Mr Cleave, a news vendor, conducting his own case before Lord Lyndhurst, began his defence by observing that he was afraid he would, before he sat down, give some rather awkward illustrations of the truth of the adage – 'he who acted as his own counsel had a fool for his client':

Ah! Mr Cleave, ah! Mr Cleave, don't you mind that adage; it was framed by the lawyers.

* * *

Lord Justice MacKinnon (1909–1946)

Describing the obscurity of parliamentary language:

The parliamentary game . . . has always been for the Government to propose Bills, and for the Opposition, by every method of debate, amendment, even obstruction, to waste time and prevent them passing. The more difficult and unintelligible a Bill is, the harder it is for the Opposition to play this game, especially if this difficulty is unintelligibility arising from the deplorable system of legislation by reference.

* * *

Lord Macmillan (1873–1952)

The life of the law has not been logic; it has been experience.

In his Observations on the Art of Advocacy *he confesses that he often used to consult* Who's Who *before addressing a parliamentary committee:*

It is unwise to attack too violently the practices of landowners when that invaluable manual has informed you that a member of the committee owns thirty thousand acres.

In Russian and English Bank v Baring Brothers:

A legal system which for so long admitted as suitors in its courts those wholly fictitious persons John Doe and

Richard Doe, who were in much worse case than the Russian and English Bank, for they never existed at all, might be expected to suffer with equanimity the apparition, at the bidding of the Legislature, of a dissolved company as a plaintiff.

There is no acquired learning, however seemingly remote from the profession, which a lawyer does not sooner or later have an opportunity of putting into practical use. . . . Some acquaintance with the less reputable side of life might have saved an Attorney General, who informed the noble and learned lords that roulette was played with cards, from suffering a devastating monosyllabic correction from the Woolsack.

* * *

Lord Mansfield (1753–1821)

Lord Mansfield's examination of an old woman, by whom he wished to prove the identity of a certain party:

MANSFIELD : Was he a tall man?

WOMAN : Not very tall, your honour – much about the size of your worship's honour.

MANSFIELD : Was he good looking?

WOMAN: Quite contrary – much like your honour; but with a handsome nose!

MANSFIELD: Did he squint?

WOMAN: A little, your worship; but not so much as your honour by a good deal!

In the habit of favouring with particular notice a certain Mr Fielding, the son of the novelist, when Fielding made his début in court he was put completely at ease by Lord Mansfield addressing him:

Well, Tom Jones, let us hear what you have got to say.

Possessed of a particular quickness in discovering the gist of a cause, having done so, he used to amuse himself by taking up a book or newspaper whilst counsel was addressing the court. One day Mr Dunning (afterwards Lord Ashburton) suddenly stopped his address and, on his lordship observing, 'Pray go on Mr Dunning.' he replied:

I beg your pardon, my lord, but I fear I shall interrupt your lordship's more important occupations. I will wait until your lordship has leisure to attend to my client and his humble advocate.

* * *

Lord Justice Mathew (1830–1908)

Of a somewhat over-emotional advocate:

When he addresses a jury, every eye in court is dry – except his own.

When Lord Justice Mathew and Mr Justice Day were on circuit together on one occasion, a high sheriff sent the latter, who was famous for his strict sentences and his love of good wine, various bottles of port from his cellar. He subsequently asked Lord Justice Mathew whether Mr Justice Day liked the wine:

As was to be expected, he tried them all patiently and punished them severely.

A new batch of 'silks' were making their bow in a Divisional Court. They did not appear a distinguished group. 'Who are all these men?' asked Lord Justice Mathew of his brother judge. 'Some of them are patent lawyers, I think,' replied his colleagues to which Mathew added:

The rest, no doubt, are latent lawyers.

* * *

Sir Theobald Mathew (b 1898)

Says that Kemp, a QC, was fond of quoting:

. . . of every hundred cases, ninety win themselves, three are won by advocacy, and seven are lost by advocacy.

* * *

Sir William Maule (1788–1858)

Addressing a jury:

Gentlemen, the learned counsel is perfectly right in his law, there is *some* evidence upon that point; but he's a lawyer, and you are not, and you do not know what he means by some evidence, so I will tell you. Suppose there was an action on a bill of exchange, and six people swore that they saw the defendant accept it, and six others swore they heard him say he should have to pay it, and six others knew him intimately, and swore to his hand-writing; and suppose on the other side, they called a poor old man, who had been at school with the defendant forty years before and had not seen him since, and he said he rather thought the statement was not his writing. Why there would be *some* evidence that it was not, and that is what Mr X means in this case.

A drunken witness, leaving the box, blurted out: 'My lord, I never cared for anything but women and horse-flesh!' Maule replied:

Then I advise you to go home and make your will, or if you have made it, put a codicil to it, and direct your executors, as soon as you are dead, to have you flayed, and to have your skin made into side saddles, and then, whatever happens, you will have the satisfaction of reflecting that, after death, some part of you will be constantly in contact with what, in life, were the dearest objects of your affection.

When, as Mr Maule, appearing before Mr Justice Taunton:

THE COURT: Mr Maule, Mr Maule – you have been arguing for the last half hour, and like a child, like a child, Mr Maule.

MR MAULE: I am well content to be likened to a child, for a child, if spared, becomes in process of time a man; but once a bear, my lord, always a brute.

THE COURT: Do you know what an oath is, my child?

SMALL GIRL: Yes, sir; I am obliged to tell the truth.

THE COURT: And if you always tell the truth where will you go when you die?

SMALL GIRL: Up to heaven, sir.

THE COURT: And what will become of you if you tell lies?

SMALL GIRL: I shall go to the naughty place, sir.

THE COURT: Are you sure of that?

SMALL GIRL: Yes, sir; quite sure.

MAULE: Let her be sworn, it is clear she knows a great deal more than I do.

On nominal damages:

In effect only a peg to hang costs on.

Upon a man being convicted for bigamy:

CLERK OF ASSIZE: What have you to say why judgment should not be passed upon you according to law?

PRISONER: Well, my lord, my wife took up with a hawker and ran away five years ago, and I have never seen her since, and I married this other woman last winter.

MR JUSTICE MAULE: I will tell you what you ought to have done; if you say you did not know, I must tell you the law conclusively presumes that you did. You ought to have instructed your attorney to bring an action against the hawker for criminal conversation with your wife. That would have cost you about a hundred pounds. When you had recovered substantial damages against the hawker, you should have instructed your proctor to sue in the ecclesiastical courts for a divorce *a mensa atque thoro*. That would have lost you two hundred or three hundred pounds more. When you had obtained a divorce *a mensa atque thoro*, you would have had to appear by counsel before the House of Lords for a divorce *a vinculo matromonii*. The bill might have been opposed in all its stages in both Houses of Parliament; and altogether you would have to have spent about one thousand or one thousand two hundred pounds. You will probably tell me that you never had a thousand farthings of your own in the world; but, prisoner, that makes no difference. Sitting here as a British judge, it is my duty to tell you that this is not a country in which there is one law for the rich and another for the poor.

*   *   *

R E Megarry (b 1910)

Commercial drafting is not always noted for its precision; nor, business men may retort, is legal drafting conspicuous for its clarity. A combination of the two styles may transcend the achievements of either.

In a Hamlyn lecture which he delivered:

A client fifty years ago laid his troubles before his solicitor and was told that there was nothing that he could do. Nevertheless, the client insisted that a writ should be issued, and persisted in this even when leading counsel advised that the case was hopeless. The case was duly lost, and as they walked away from the court, the client said: 'Where do we go from here?' The solicitor said: 'Well, you can go to the Court of Appeal, but I don't advise it'. The client replied: 'Appeal!' and in due course promptly paid the solicitor's bill without demur.

The appeal was duly lost, and in a similar way the bill was paid and an appeal to the House of Lords was lost. As they walked away from the House of Lords, the client said: 'Where do we go from here?' The solicitor replied: 'You can't go anywhere. The Lords are final. Only a private Act of Parliament could alter the result.' Whereupon the client said: 'Commence proceedings for a private Act.'

The solicitor stopped dead in his tracks, and looked at his client with admiration: 'My dear sir,' he said, 'I should like to breed from you.'

In the same lecture he also gave thanks to modern improvements in court furniture:

As an aside, I may perhaps add a word of gratitude for the rubber padding that has quite recently found its way on to most, if not all, of the seats in counsel's rows at the Law

Courts. In my junior days another of the techniques of the bar was learning how to endure a plain wooden seat for two daily sessions of nearly two and a half hours each. Nature has not endowed all counsel equally in this respect, and although the years brought their ischial callosities, psychologically if not physiologically, prevention is better than endurance.

I hope the phrase 'benevolent spider' will not give offence; but that is how the function of a solicitor may best be represented. He sits in the middle of his web and pulls each of the radial cords as need dictates.

After all, the cynics say, the real triumph for counsel is not so much to win the case but to win the solicitors who instructed his opponent.

* * *

David Napley (b 1915)

About the introduction of majority verdicts into England, as are now used in Scotland:

The haggis, which has worked well there, has never, thank God, found acceptance here, and a majority amongst fifteen jurors in a small community may well provide a better safeguard than a majority among only twelve in a large one.

* * *

Lord Norbury (1740–1831)

When charging a jury, he was interrupted by the braying of a donkey: 'What noise is that?' cried Lord Norbury:

Tis only the echo of the court, my lord.

The registrar of one of the Irish criminal courts complained to Lord Norbury that the witnesses were in the habit of stealing the Testament after they had been sworn upon it:

Never mind, if the rascals read the book it will do them more good than the petty larceny will do them mischief. However, if they are not afraid of cord, hang your books in chains, and that, perhaps by reminding the fellows of the fate of their fathers and grandfathers, will make them behave themselves.

* * *

Lord Northington (1708–1786)

George III used to relate the way in which Northington asked permission to abolish the Chancellor's evening sittings on Wednesdays and Fridays during term, in order that he might have time to finish his bottle. His excesses in this way subjected him to repeated and severe attacks of gout, and when suffering he was heard to mutter to himself, while walking from the Woolsack to the bar:

If I had known these legs of mine were meant to carry a Lord Chancellor, I would have taken better care of them when I was a boy.

* * *

Lord du Parcq (1880–1949)

When Chairman of the Royal Commission on Justices of the Peace of 1947, referring to the retirement age for justices:

You see, you and I have known judges who have sat well over the age of eighty and who have been extraordinarily good. On the other hand, if we were alone we should probably admit to each other that we have known judges at the age of sixty who might well have retired.

I think the cases are comparatively few in which much light is obtained by a liberal use of Latin phrases . . . Nobody can derive any assistance from the phrase, *novus actus interveniens* until it is translated into English, and, if the judge is going to sum up a case to a jury, I think that, by the time he has done, he will probably find he could have got on equally well without it.

Speaking of solicitors:

The first rule is: never believe anything they say in your instructions until you have verified it for yourself.

* * *

A P Pennell (1867–1947)

A renowned 'Ancient' of the Middle Temple, towards the end of his life, he steadfastly refused to leave his chambers at the top of Lamb's Building during the worst days of the blitz. In vain wardens implored him to come down to shelter. When the first bomb fell on the Inner Temple Hall, adjoining Lamb's Building, the wardens rushed up the staircase and hammered on his oaken door. For a long time there was no response. Then a dishevelled old figure with rumpled hair slowly opened the door and asked what all the fuss was about. 'You must come down at once.' 'I am quite comfortable where I am,' Pennell replied. 'But you must come, it is impossible to stay here any longer.' 'Why?' 'A bomb has just landed on the Inner Temple Hall and knocked it to pieces':

I *thought* I heard a noise.

Dining one night at the 'Ancient's Table' of the Middle Temple was a stickler for the benchers maintaining those customs and privileges of the Inn pertaining to the ancients. On an occasion when the only two benchers dining in Hall, Lords Craigmyle and Salvesen, passed down the Hall after dinner deep in conversation, oblivious altogether of the ancients at their table, and thus failed to bestow a special bow on the senior ancient – Pennell – the old stickler was upset and disturbed and muttered to Pennell:

Never mind, they're only Scots.

* * *

Lord Phillimore (1845–1929)

A man was being tried before Lord Phillimore at the Leeds Assizes for the murder of his wife. 'Did you say to your wife: "If you don't bloody well take care you will repent of it"?' the prisoner was asked. 'No, I couldn't have said that, I don't use that word,' he replied. 'I suppose,' interposed Lord Phillimore, 'it is the word beginning with b that you do not use?' :

Oh no! I do use that word. It's the word repent which I don't use!

He did not believe strongly in divorce, and refused when called upon to make a number of decrees nisi granted in the divorce division. This provoked the comment by the President of the PDA (Probate, Divorce and Admiralty) Division at that time:

Here is my brother Phillimore, who objects to making decrees nisi absolute because he believes in the sanctity of marriage. No doubt we will soon have a Unitarian appointed to the bench, who will refuse to try Admiralty suits, as he would have to sit with the Trinity masters.

In sentencing a burglar, Lord Phillimore referred to him as a 'professional', to which the prisoner strongly protested from the dock. ' 'Ere,' he exclaimed, 'I dunno wot you mean by callin' me a professional burglar. I've only done it once before, an' I've been nabbed both times' :

Oh, I did not mean to say that you had been very successful in your profession.

* * *

Lord Pollock (1823–1897)

Sitting in a court on circuit, he was disturbed by the bells of a nearby church:

I was not aware that this was a Court of Appeal.

He was known as a merciful judge, and criminals were always very pleased when he tried their case. The chaplain of a prison had managed to work a repentant sinner into such a state of mind that he had decided to plead guilty, by way of small reparation to society for his offence. When arraigned at the bar, he pleaded not guilty and was acquitted. The chaplain asked him why, in view of his promise, he had done so:

Well, your reverence, I did intend to plead guilty and take my punishment, and mend my ways, but, Lord bless you, I never guessed that it was to be the Lord Chief Baron. As soon as I clapped my eyes on the dear old boy I know'd I had a good chance, and so I up an' said, 'Not guilty, my lord,' and I knew by his look he meant to get me off. If they was all like him it would be better times for us!

* * *

Lord Reading (1860–1935)

While still an advocate, Rufus Isaacs (later Lord Reading) was presumptuously propounding the law on the issues raised. Lord Justice Vaughan Williams broke in upon him:

Wait a little, Mr Isaacs, till you come up here on the bench as you undoubtedly will!

* * *

Lord Reid (b 1890)

I am certainly not going to attempt a definition of capital expenditure on the one hand or of revenue expenditure on the other. Like most ordinary English words or expressions they are probably incapable of exact definition.

* * *

Crabb Robinson (1766–1833)

Just called to the bar, he told Charles Lamb exultantly that he was retained in a cause in the King's Bench, to which Lamb remarked:

Ah, the first great cause, least understood.

* * *

Mr Justice Roxburgh (b 1889)

It is never safe to construe an Act of Parliament by paying undue attention to the meaning of the words.

* * *

Lord Russell (b 1908)

To the comparative newcomer, the law of libel seems to have characteristics of such complication and subtlety that I wonder whether a jury on retiring can readily distinguish their heads from their heals.

I have an uneasy feeling that on this point my judgment is to that of Lord Justice Diplock, as Watson was to Holmes, and that it may merit the sub-title 'Rattle of a Simple Man'; but there it is.

If a man threw a tomato at me in court, I would not consider his character. I would send him straight to prison.

* * *

Mr Justice Scarman (b 1911)

A nominal award (damages for adultery) is out of the question, for the loss and injury are substantial, though immeasurable. A conventional award . . . is also wrong, for it would fail to provide the solatium which is the most that the law can offer, and might subject the law to ridicule – 'a tariff for adulterers (male)'.

* * *

John Selden (1584–1654)

Little things doe great workes, when great things will not. If I would take upp a pinn from the ground, a little paire of Tongues will doe it, when a great paire will not; goe to a Judge to do a business for you, by no means as he will not heare of it, but goe to some small sarveant about him, and he will dispatch it, according to your hearts desire.

Though some make slight of Libells, yet you may see by them how the wind setts; as, take a straw, and throw it upp into the aire, you shall see by that which way the wind is, which you shall not doe by casting upp a stone – More solid things doe not shew the complexion of the times so well as Ballads and Libells.

The King of Spaine was Outlaw'd in Westminster hall, I being of Councell against him. A merchant had recovered costs against the King of Spaine in a suite, which because it could not be gott, we advised to have him outlaw'd for his not appearing, and so hee was, As soon as Gondimar heard that, he presently sent the money, by reason if his Master had stood outlaw'd he could not have had the benefit of the Law which would have been very prejudiciall, there being then many suites depending betwixt the King of Spaine and our English Merchants.

* * *

Thomas Sewell (d 1784)

In 1764, in a House of Commons debate Sir Charles Sewell, Master of the Rolls, said, when a motion was put for a three-day adjournment to consider a particular subject, that such an adjournment would enable him to look into the authorities and give a decided opinion on the subject, which he was at present unable to do. The adjournment was carried, and when the debate was resumed after it he said that he had that morning turned the whole matter over in his mind as he lay upon his pillow, and after ruminating and considering a great deal he could not help declaring that he was of the same opinion that he was before. Upon this Charles Townsend started up and exclaimed that:

He was very sorry to observe that what the right honourable gentleman had found in his nightcap he had lost in his periwig.

* * *

Sir Launcelot Shadwell (1799–1850)

When Vice Chancellor of England he declared in his evidence before the Chancery Commission that the business in the court was so heavy:

That three angels would not get through it.

* * *

Lord Simon (1873–1954)

In an appreciation of Lord MacKinnon (who died in 1946) he told of the author's delight on hearing that his (MacKinnon's) book ON CIRCUIT *was classified in a local library:*

As a treatise on electricity.

The profession of the bar is not a bed of roses, for it is either all bed and no roses, or else all roses and no bed.

Taking silk consists of making one's head very hot in an absurdly large and heavy wig, and one's legs very cold with absurdly thin and very draughty stockings.

* * *

Lord Simonds (b 1881)

On this question counsel on either side agreed in saying that there was no direct authority and they agreed too that the reason for that was that the answer was clear. But unfortunately here harmony ended, for the clear answer given on the one side was the exact opposite of the clear answer given on the other.

It is, no doubt, desirable that the same meaning should be given to the same word whenever it is used in a statute, though a long experience of statutes has left me with some scepticism on that principle.

I deprecate any tendency to treat the relation of employer and skilled workman as equivalent to that of nurse and imbecile child.

. . . I need hardly add that, as is usual in such cases, each side invokes the plain ordinary meaning of the English language, and claims that, judged by that test, the words can bear only one, but a different, interpretation.

* * *

Lord Justice Singleton (1885–1957)

When examining the photograph of a scene of an accident:

Is that the oldest inhabitant watching?

Counsel explained that it was in fact:

Not a very good photograph of my instructing solicitor.

* * *

Mr Justice Stable (b 1888)

Addressing the jury in a case of alleged obscene libel:

. . . you know that babies of either sex are not born into this world dressed up in a frock coat or an equivalent feminine garment . . . in the Victorian era . . . in some houses legs of tables were actually draped and rather stricter females, never referred to a gentleman's legs as such but, called them their 'understandings'.

During a slander action he assured a woman witness that:

Although I look very odd in these clothes, I do spend the rest of the time in the world in which we both live, and I know something about village life and life elsewhere. Just you think you are having a good gossip with me over a cup of tea.

* * *

Sir Thomas Strutton (1856–1934)

Describing goodwill:

The cat prefers the old home to the person who keeps it, and stays in the old home though the person who has kept the house leaves. The cat represents that part of the customers who continue to go to the old shop, though the old shopkeeper has gone; the probability of their custom may be regarded as an additional value given to the premises by the tenant's trading. The dog represents that part of the customers who follow the person rather than the place; these the tenant may take away with him if he does not go too far. There remains a class of customer who may neither follow the place nor the person, but drift away elsewhere. They are neither a benefit to the landlord nor the tenant, and have been called 'the rat' for no particular reason except to keep the epigram in the animal kingdom. I believe my brother Maugham has introduced the rabbit, but I will leave him to explain the position of the rabbit.

It is an excellent rule not to go, for the purposes of your decision, beyond what is necessary.

A King's Bench judge who deals with juries soon learns that the fact that he takes a particular view does not mean that no other is reasonable.

* * *

Lord Thurlow (1731–1806)

Lord Thurlow was noted for his outbursts of swearing and Campbell in his LORD CHANCELLORS OF ENGLAND *says:*

I have been told by an old gentleman who was standing behind the Woolsack at the time, that Sir Ilay Campbell, then Lord Advocate, arguing a Scots appeal at the bar in a very tedious manner, said: 'I will noo, my lords, proceed to my seventh point.' 'I'll be damned if you do!' cried Thurlow, so as to be heard by all present. 'This House is adjourned until Monday next.' And off he scampered.

But one retort he received conveyed to him a salutory hint of the ultimate consequences of his habit of swearing: He was one morning put into a great rage by finding that a cartload of paving stones had been shot before his door for the purpose of repairing the street. Observing an Irish paviour near the heap, he addressed himself in a furious tone at the culprit and ordered him to remove them:

IRISH PAVIOUR: Where shall I take them to, please your honour?

LORD THURLOW: To hell and be damned to you!

IRISH PAVIOUR: If I were to take them to t'other place, your honour, don't you think they might be more out of your honour's way?

*   *   *

Judge Tudor-Rees (d 1956)

WITNESS: The gentleman is a JP not an MP.

JUDGE TUDOR-REES: The difference between a JP and an MP, I believe, is one thousand pounds a year.

* * *

Mr Justice Vaisey (1877–1965)

Witnesses who are not lawyers are usually much better witnesses.

* * *

Lord Webb-Johnson (1880–1958)

In a letter to The Times *headed 'Physical Discomfiture of Litigation':*

I wonder if there is any reason why those who attend the Royal Courts of Justice should have only a wooden bench to sit on. Litigants, who often have to be present for several successive days and are providing the cost of the proceedings, suffer serious discomfort from their long sojourn on the antiquated perches provided. It is true that barristers and solicitors have to put up with similar hard benches, but at least they are paid for doing so. With long practice, moreover, they may find some way of securing a moderate degree of comfort or acquire immunity from damage by developing ischial callosities like baboons, who sit on barren rocks. I feel sure, however, that a little upholstery would be welcomed by all.

* * *

Joshua West (18th century)

Will of Joshua West of the Six Clerks' Office, Chancery Lane:

Perhaps I died not worth a groat;
But should I die worth something more,
Then I give that, and my best coat,
And all my manuscripts in store,
To those who shall the goodness have
To cause my poor remains to rest
Within a decent shell and grave.
This is the will of Joshua West.

* * *

John Wilkes (1727–1792)

Horne Took challenged John Wilkes, who was at the time Sheriff of London and Middlesex, and received the reply:

I do not think it my business to cut the throat of every desperado that may be tired of his life; but as I am at present High Sheriff of the City of London, it may happen that I shall shortly have an opportunity of attending you in my official capacity, in which case I will answer for it that you shall have no ground to complain of my endeavours to serve you.

*   *   *

Lord Vaughan Williams (1838–1916)

A Mr Cook, QC, who was a very self-assured advocate, had just finished with a witness, when Lord Justice Vaughan Williams put a question to him, at the same time asking Mr Cook why he hadn't asked it. 'I was much inclined to do so, my lord, but I felt rather nervous':

And pray, Mr Cook, how did you enjoy the sensation?

During a midday adjournment, when he was acting as Judge in Chambers, he began to leave without taking his hat. His janitor, noticing this, remarked, 'My lord, here's your hat. Don't leave it here or you mayn't find it when you come back.' Not usually paying much attention to sartorial matters, and more in sorrow than in anger, the judge answered: 'Do you think anyone would take that hat?' Looking at the headgear more carefully, the janitor replied thoughtfully:

Now you mention it, I think you can leave it here quite safely!

* * *

Lord Justice Willmer (b 1899)

I am aware that the practice of attaching epithets to the word 'cause' has been frowned on by no less an authority than Lord Sumner . . . but at least one may be permitted to hold that a cause is something which causes.

* * *

Mr Justice Wills (1828–1912)

A barrister was wasting the time of the court with a long-winded speech. He dealt at unnecessary length with the appearance of certain bags which were used in evidence. 'They might,' he went on pompously, 'they might have been full bags, or they might have been half-filled bags, or they might have been empty bags, or—':

Or perhaps, *interpolated Judge Wills,* they might have been wind-bags!

* * *

Mr Justice Winn (b 1903)

On three defendants in a case:

McGuinness had in his pocket an unloaded starting pistol ... Edwards had a piece of lead piping in his trousers pocket ... Salisbury had in his trouser pocket a hammer shaft – none of these articles can have assisted the set of the young men's clothing very much.

On being informed that a youth could only dance slow waltzes since being injured:

Perhaps he will meet a better type of partner in the slow foxtrot than in the twist.

* * *

Anonymous

A certain judge at an Assize sat in a building sometimes used for concerts, and was respectfully told that there was to be a performance there of The Messiah, *and that it was hoped to hold a rehearsal some time on the day the court sat. His lordship indicated that, subject to the requirements of justice, he would not sit late on that day. When his clerk later drew attention to the time, his lordship replied:*

The Messiah must wait.

The three deadly sins which cause domestic upheaval and lead to the Divorce Court are, according to the Secretary of the Poor Persons Committee of the Law Society in 1945, selfishness, jealousy and lodgers.

Counsel to a medical expert giving evidence:

You will admit that doctors do make mistakes, won't you?

Yes, the same as lawyers.

But doctors' mistakes are buried underground.

Yes, but lawyers' mistakes are left swinging in the air.

During a cross-examination in a case brought against the Costa Brava Wine Company Limited:

COUNSEL: The poor man can have his white sparkling wine, but he cannot have champagne because it is always expensive. You want to keep the snobbish value of champagne as a rich man's wine. Why cannot he have his poor man's champagne?

WITNESS: You might as well say why can't margarine be called butter so that the poor man can have butter.

By Atticus, the Sunday Times *columnist, about a judge in the time of rationing in 1947, who took 'a little packet' into the dining room of his London Club:*

He opened it at the table, took out two small pieces of bread, and began his dinner. When he had finished his soup and his meat course he ordered a savoury. The waiter said politely, but firmly: I'm afraid you can't have it, sir. You've had bread, and bread counts as a course.' The judge looked up and explained: 'But you have not served me; I'm eating my own bread.' The waiter hesitated, retired to seek advice, and came back with the same answer, the bread counted as a course. This time the judge became judicial: 'You will serve me my savoury, and, if you are not satisfied, you can report me to the Ministry of Food. If they bring a case, I shall conduct my own defence!'

The Committee on Mechanical Recording of Court Proceedings recently issued an interim report on its findings. Among its observations was:

Microphones can of course pick up talk which does not and is not intended to reach the judge.

Man is an able creature, but he has made 35,643,692 laws and hasn't yet improved on the Ten Commandments.

Defendant in a County Court action: 'As God is my judge, I did not take the money':

JUDGE: He isn't. I am. You did.

A little boy was brought before a magistrate, charged with throwing stones at passing railway trains. 'What have you to say,' asked the judge. 'I didn't throw no stones, sir, I was only going to.' 'Only going to!' echoed the magistrate. 'Well, the intent was there, and as a deterrent I shall fine you five pounds.'

The father took the youngster by the hand and proceeded to leave the courtroom when the magistrate called him back and reminded him that he had failed to pay the fine:

That's quite so, I should have done so; but as the intent is just as good in the eyes of the law, why, you're paid.

Barristers on opposite sides of a case are like the two parts of shears; they cut what comes between them but not each other.

A young barrister had been talking for about four hours to a jury who, when he had finished, felt somewhat exhausted. His opponent then arose and, looking sweetly at the judge, said:

My lord, I will follow the example of my friend who has just finished and submit the case without argument.

'Judge,' said the prisoner, 'I don't know what to do.'

'Why, what is the matter,' asked the judge.

'I swore to tell the truth, but every time I try some lawyer objects.'

A man was facing trial and possible imprisonment. 'I know the evidence is against me,' he told his lawyer, 'but I've got twenty thousand pounds in cash to fight this case.' 'You'll never go to prison with that amount of money,' the lawyer assured him:

He didn't. He went there broke.

LAWSUIT – a machine which you go into as a pig and come out of as a sausage.

JURY – Twelve men who are chosen to decide which of the parties has the better barrister.

LAWYER – Shrewdest distance between two points.

– A person who helps you get what's coming to him.

– He who is summoned when the felon needs a friend.

– A fellow who is willing to give all and spend your last cent to prove he's right.

A businessman who had consulted his solicitor for some legal advice ran into an acquaintance to whom he recounted his experience. 'But why spend money for a lawyer?' the friend asked. 'Didn't you see all those law books while you sat in his office? Well, the answers were all there. What he told you, you could easily have read for yourself in those very books and you would have saved having to pay a big fee' :

Yes, that's all very true. The only difference is that the lawyer knows what page it's on.

A lawyer had his portrait taken in his favourite attitude – standing with his hands in his pockets. It was remarked that the portrait would have been more like the lawyer if it had represented him with his hands in another man's pockets, instead of his own.

A policeman, giving evidence on an encounter with a drunken motorist, quoted the motorist as saying:

I know, I know, anything I say will be taken down in writing, altered, and used in evidence against me.

At the end of a trial on indictment at the Old Bailey, a prisoner was asked by the judge if he had anything to say why sentence should not be passed upon him:

THE PRISONER: — all!
THE JUDGE (*to the associate*): What did he say?
THE ASSOCIATE: He said '— all', my lord.
THE JUDGE: That's funny, I thought he said something.

QUESTION: Why is the figure of Justice over the Old Bailey blindfold?
ANSWER: So as not to see her many miscarriages.

A judge interrupted learned counsel who was appearing for a drunken motorist:

I think, Mr Smith, that your submissions would be more effective if you were to put your wig on straight.

On the four Inns of Court:

Inner for the rich man,
Middle for the poor.
Lincoln's for the black man,
Gray's Inn for the whore.

PRISON WARDER (*to released convict*): I'm sorry. I find we have kept you here a week too long.

CONVICT: That's all right, sir. Knock it off next time.

JUDGE: Your wife says you keep her continually terrorised.

PRISONER: But, honestly, your honour—?

JUDGE: Now, not in my official capacity, but as man to man, what is your system?

Here lies a lawyer,
  Laugh if you will,
In mercy, kind Providence
  Let him lie still.
He lied for his living,
  He lived while he lied.
When he couldn't lie longer,
  He lied down and died.

Woman juror to eleven exasperated men jurors:

If you men weren't so stubborn we could all go home!

JUDGE: What possible excuse did you fellows have for acquitting that murderer.

JURYMAN: Insanity.

JUDGE: Really? All twelve of you?

A young man was brought up in court on a charge of robbery. The case against him had been closed and no testimony was forthcoming from the defendant. The judge turned to him impatiently: 'Where are your witnesses? Haven't you any witnesses in this case?' The prisoner, somewhat bewildered, replied:

Witnesses? Not me. I never take along any witnesses when I commit a robbery.

A lawyer was drawing up papers of partnership for two manufacturers. He went over the papers before the final signing, but he found them incomplete. 'There is no mention here,' he said, 'of fire or bankruptcy. These must go in':

Quite right, *said the partners, speaking together*; put them in, but the profits are to be divided equally in both cases.

LAWYER (*handing cheque for one hundred pounds to client who had been awarded five hundred pounds*): There's the balance after deducting my fee. What are you thinking of? Aren't you satisfied?

CLIENT: I was just wondering who got hit by the car, you or I.

Barrister to all male jury:

Gentlemen, shall this charming young lady be cast into a lonely cell, or shall she return to her beautiful little flat at 34 Wilson Avenue, telephone 349-6814.

THE COURT: Why do you wish a new trial for your client?

COUNSEL: On the grounds of newly discovered matter, your honour.

THE COURT: And what is the nature of that?

COUNSEL: My client has dug up some money that I didn't know he had!

PROFESSOR OF LAW: If you have the facts on your side, hammer them into the jury, and if you have the law on your side, hammer it into the judge.

STUDENT: But if you have neither the facts nor the law?

PROFESSOR: Then hammer on the table.

'So you fought with this man because he said your wife was the ugliest woman in town?' asked the judge of the man brought before him on a charge of disturbing the peace. 'Why you haven't even got a wife' :

Yes, sir, I know, but I was just fighting for the principle of the thing.

JUDGE (*looking at a defendant who was unscathed after a serious car accident*) : It must feel pretty good to be alive.

DEFENDANT : I don't know, judge, I've never been dead.

JUDGE : You are accused of stealing a chicken. Anything to say?

PRISONER : Just took it for a lark, sir.

JUDGE : No resemblance whatever. Ten days.

Barrister : 'I must tell you before the case comes on that it would have been better had you acted more on defensive lines. If you had not struck first you would have had the law on your side.' The man, who was suing his neighbour for what he termed a murderous attack, shook his head disgustedly :

Perhaps I would 'ave 'ad the law on my side, but, at the same time, I should 'ave 'ad his blinkin' boot in me jaw.

A man charged with murder consulted a famous barrister but bulked at the proposed fee, saying that another barrister had offered to defend him for much less:

I would suggest that you retain this other fellow. He will charge you half the fee and you won't even have to pay it. Your heirs will.

A little bird told me what kind of lawyer your father was.
What did the bird say?
Cheep, cheep.
Well. A duck told me what kind of a doctor your old man was.

Dialogue between a learned Serjeant and a learned Baron of the Exchequer while on circuit. Upon the Serjeant entering the court one morning the judge said in a sharp voice:

Brother, you are late – the court has wasted a considerable time.

I beg your pardon, my lord. I was not aware that your lordship intended sitting so early. The instant I heard your lordship's trumpet I dressed myself.

You were a long time about it, brother.

I think, my lord, not twenty minutes.

Twenty minutes, Mr Serjeant! I was ready in five minutes after I left my bed.

In that respect my dog, Shock, distances your lordship hollow; he only shakes his coat and fancies himself sufficiently dressed for any company.

During the long war with Republican and Imperial France, the lawyers formed two corps of volunteers, which were respectively nicknamed the 'Devil's Own' and the 'Devil's Invincibles'. Attorneys were admitted to the ranks of the latter, and when Colonel Cox, the Master in Chancery, who commanded the Corps gave the word 'Charge!' it is said that two-thirds of his rank and file took out their note books and wrote down 6s. 8d.

The Court in charge:

The prosecutrix in this case is an unfortunate woman. At least she says she is an unfortunate woman, and we all know what an unfortunate woman is; at least I know; so do you I think; so does everyone in court.

The court to witness:

You must remember, and if you don't remember you ought to know, that nothing whatever that is said in a prisoner's absence against him can be used in evidence under any circumstances whatever if he was not present when it was said; and if he was, any man might be convicted and hanged in five minutes.

PRISONER: I want to ask whether it is likely . . .

THE COURT: We have nothing to do with what is likely or unlikely; so many unlikely things happen in courts of justice that the public time should not be wasted on such enquiries.

The court in charge: If ever there was a case of clearer evidence than this of persons acting together, this case is that case.

A forger is a fellow who gives a cheque a bad name.

Old lawyers never die. They just lose their appeal.